For Clare & Matthew.
love you
(today & everyday after that)

- Rachel x

Also with a special Big love to all my Amazing family &
friends who make every Today the best One ever.

A TEMPLAR BOOK

First published in the UK in 2012 by Templar Publishing,
an imprint of The Templar Company Limited,
The Granary, North Street, Dorking, Surrey, RH4 1DN, UK
www.templarco.co.uk

ISBN 978-1-84877-487-2

Printed in the U.K.

ToDaY
is going to Be the
Best Day
EVer

Super
little
mini-WiSdOms
On
SUCCESS
fROm

the bright side

May I suggest starting the day with a morning...

SUCCESS MANTRA

Yes repeat after me...

I will be **BOLD**.
I will be generous.
I will be as true to myself as I can possibly be.
I will Change
the World (even just
a tiny bit)
&
TRIUMPH over adversity.

I will
Strut my stuff
(particularly when it's funky)

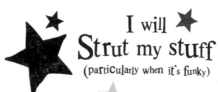

& Have the luck of the Irish.*
(*Especially if I am actually Irish)

I will Float like a butterfly

& Sting like a bee.

I will pump up the Volume
& Without exception, I will
Treat everyday like a Special occasion
& every person like a V.I.P.
(including of course, my very good Self).

I shall do Some good deeds

& Hug

& file (like a demon)
& Learn impressive new facts & generally
GO FOR IT.

Yes, I will
GRAB LIFE
BY THE ROUND THINGS.*

*But not so hard as to cause permanent damage.

And more than that I will… Have Unshakeable confidence,

Bounce, Leap, Run, Skip, Splash & generally feel Spring in my soul (whatever the season).

I won't talk with my Mouth full, but I will speak with my mind OPEN & I will Ponder the Universe.

I will Laugh till my tummy hurts as often as possible…

thank my lucky Stars & see magic everywhere.

Whilst being all impromptu,

I will imagine what I would do if
anything
was possible & then
DO IT

I will Look Forward
& never back (unless I am
reversing).
I shall forget to worry & regularly
practise my evil laugh
(Mwha ha ha ha).
I shall know that EVERYTHING
wonderful is coming my way...

& I will always try to look on
the bright side.

Aim for the MOoN*

*The **Rock** in the **Sky** rather than the **Cheeks** in the **minibus** window

Be
Strangers to
Convention,
Breakers of
Rules &
Flouters of Boundaries.
Be Explorers Of
tHe
World.*

Z
Z
Z
Z
Z
Z
Z
Z

*Also, occasionally, be sitters on the sofa & havers of naps.

RECIPE for

You my friend are the CHEF of SUCCESS.
The ARTIST of ACHIEVEMENT. The MAESTRO of MOJO.
May you mix up life to the perfect CONSISTENCY
& cook up EVERYTHING YOU WANT:

INGREDIENTS

1. One twinkle in your eye
2. A healthy dose of CHARISMA
3. Three dollops of fruity passion
4. A big wedge of teeth (otherwise known as a Smile)
5. A Sprinkle of LOVeliness
6. A chunk of Confidence
7. Chocolate*

*Ok you don't really need
Chocolate, but you know, Why not?

SUCCESS

Once you have all these things,
the method is easy :

1. Great everything
2. Need it all together
3. Blend with plenty of FUN
4. Know that for things to go right in the end, sometimes they have to go a bit wrong in the beginning
5. Add a bit of HEAT (you old devil)
6. Watch as your creation RISES
7. Savour your success with some sort of biscuit

Evil plans for

Whether your dream today is simple - like, I don't know, having a good day at the office, or something maHOOsive like swimming with sharks (you crazy kid), it pays to take note of what the successful heroes & villains of this world have in common - then try them out to see if it works for you...

Stand with hands on hips & determined look in your eye

Have a Secret HideOut (preferably under a mountain)

Have a Catchphrase

Try teaming a cape with your usual daywear - see if you can pull off the look

World Domination*

*& also some non-evil ones

Laugh like you are a bit mad

Show no fear

Use excessive Hair Styling products

Stroke your facial hair pensively (girls try eyebrow smoothing)

Always bounce back

Have a Sidekick

LaUGh in tHe FaCe of Fear*

*With the One exception of angry tigers. In that Scenario I would advise fairly brisk running.

& If you are ever unsure of your direction in life...

Spend some time sitting quietly in the forest of your mind & you will soon know the way to go. Too often we get lost randomly chasing the squirrels of distraction.*

*Mind
you –
the odd
random
squirrel-
chase is
quite
fun.

The ESSENTIAL SUCCESS KIT

If you want to be UBERLY successful, never leave home without the following:

Loveliness*

*Despite what the dragons would have you believe, lovely is always lucky.

A bone-crushing handshake

STYLE
(Can include: bling, shoulder enhancement & a hat)

Listen to Chariots of Fire REALLY LOUDLY (extra points for slow motion running)

Write 'And the Award goes to…' at the top of your bedroom mirror & practise your acceptance Speech

Be enthusiastic (to the point of popping a Vein)

Make mistakes. Shake things up REGULARLY & say."Hello Mr Change… I love you!"

Close your eyes. punch the air hard & Shout. "YESSsssss!"

Steps to Super-ness

Don't take NO for an answer

Get Out of your Comfort Zone

Hone a magnetic PULL & always PUSH yourself

Spend a whole day pretending you are already where you want to be.*
(*Especially if you want to be living it up 5-star stylee)

Break the rules & banish convention

make the imPOSSiBLE
POSSiBLE.
Think the
UntHinKaBLE.

EAT
the
UneataBLe.

And know that...

GOod
things
cOme to
thOse WhO
Wait *

*Good things also come
to those who don't wait.
Only quicker

Above all...

Remember that Leaps are Best taken Boldly & Quickly*

*& also Sometimes Wearing only skimpy swimwear

Yes whateVer it is you decide to do TODAY go forth & Be AMAZING (Even more amazing than you already are)